Your Ultimate Best

Create a Roadmap
to a Healthy, Happier,
More Fulfilled
Balanced Life

1ˢᵗ Edition

By: Jim Hickey

Published in 2013 by
Your Ultimate Best Ltd.

Copyright© Jim Hickey 2013

ISBN: 978-0-9926014-0-9

Printed in Ireland
by Walsh Colour Print,
Tralee Rd, Castleisland, Co. Kerry

Acknowledgments

This book springs from my passionate desire and powerful love to help people reach their true potential and live the life they deserve.

My heartfelt gratitude goes out to everyone who has helped, supported and guided me throughout my life.

Thank you,

Jim

Table of Contents

Introduction 1

Chapter 1   My Questions to You 5

Chapter 2   Action 25

Chapter 3   Life Balance Wheel 33

Chapter 4   Perfect Health 37

Chapter 5   Career 41

Chapter 6   Best Partner / Best Self / Relationship 45

Chapter 7   Best Parent 49

Chapter 8   Best Son / Daughter / Brother / Sister 55

Chapter 9   Friends, Fun and Contribution 59

Chapter 10 Putting it all together 61

Further Support 68

Introduction

Many people ask me how I became a professional peak performance coach. I have always had a fascination with the power of the mind. Being self employed from a very early age, I have always had a gut instinct, that you have to believe in what you want to achieve. By having a continuous curiosity of what people have done before me has gotten me to where I am today.

From my on-going studies, I realize that all of our answers lie within us and for these answers to emerge we need to constantly question ourselves and allow ourselves to be questioned. I now understand that the more specific these questions are the better the results!

One of my biggest and greatest lessons is to learn from our mistakes. I have asked these next two questions over and over again from my clients:

"What was **good** about an event / situation / relationship"?
"What could be **even better** about it"?

This is my fundamental philosophy in coaching.

However, this wasn't always the person I was. Many years ago, I was blessed to have the opportunity to take on and explore the world of coaching. Previously, I would continuously get distracted with internal frustrations and challenges of mixed emotions, disappointments and other peoples motivations.

My fascination with other people's interactions, behaviours and motivations led me on the road to where I am now. I was filled with questions. I found the answer to these questions once I delved into my own journey of self-development.

From being coached myself, I have discovered that you coach a whole person - under the umbrella of warmth and respect. Thanks to the carefully crafted questions by my coach, I was able to identify and express my thoughts while feeling safe in this area. These correctly timed questions created massive shifts in my life both mentally and emotionally.

I was reared at a time when children were not encouraged to speak out and say exactly how they were feeling whether good or bad. I then realized how much my own ability to express myself hadn't fully developed. This wonderful world of coaching as well as being coached was filling needs I didn't even know existed.

I can think back to many times I asked my own coach how she became a coach.

Her answer was, Jim I qualified!

After a short time I found myself in college on the way to becoming qualified as a coach myself. Having being immersed in the world of coaching for many years previous to starting my studies, college was a nirvana for me. I was hungry for every bit of knowledge, every tool, technique and skill I could get my hands on.

At this time, I also became even more certain of my mission in life:

"CONTINUOUSLY IMPROVE MY LIFE AND THE LIVES OF AS MANY PEOPLE AS POSSIBLE"

This is my deep burning passion that drives me daily and helps me jump out of bed at 5 a.m., five mornings a week to start my day with both energy and enthusiasm.

My passion has helped me in helping other people achieve their dreams and bring them beyond what they believe is possible. Clients have told me that it is my infectious appetite for helping that helps to drive them along. By holding people continuously accountable on a regular basis, I see the results shine through.

When I get calls from people who want to bring their lives to the next level, from that moment on they share a piece of my mind.

This book is your call to me, and my way of reaching those who have not yet called me. The joy and satisfaction I get from seeing people unlock, unblock and reach their potential is phenomenal.

Chapter 1
My Questions to You

In order to find out about where you are in life, I would love to ask you some questions. These questions will create a thought process. Use this precious time to think wisely and answer these questions honestly.

When I ask these questions of my clients, their lives stand still while working on them which enables them take a "helicopter view", on each area of their lives.

These questions are for the most important person in the world… **YOU!**

On a scale of 1 to 10, can you answer the following questions on where you are, at this moment on your journey. Can you fill in your answers and then we may begin.

Are you ready to achieve what you want in your life?

Do you know what you want to achieve in your life?

I ask you to be relaxed and present while answering these questions!

Please turn the page to begin your journey.

1) Are you performing to the best of your ability?

2) Do you take the best advice?

3) Are you having your 'AHA' moments?

4) Have you gone all the way to the top?

5) Are you aware of your awesome ability?

6) Are you aligned with your true self?

7) Are you active?

_____
_____
_____

8) Are you authentic?

_____
_____
_____

9) Do you believe in yourself?

_____
_____
_____

10) Are you blooming?

_____
_____
_____

11) Are you behaving to your best?

_____
_____
_____

12) Is your life in balance?

_____
_____
_____

13) Do you follow your bliss?

14) Are your boxes being ticked?

15) Are you building your skills?

16) Is your life buzzing?

17) Are you feeling better every day?

18) Every day are you challenging yourself to be your best?

19) Are you spending time out of your comfort zone?

_____
_____
_____

When a client or friend comes to me, they want to change, improve, better themselves to be more and do more.

My question to you is, do you want this!

1) Are you in control of your life?

_____
_____
_____

2) Are you continuing to make changes?

_____
_____
_____

3) Are you making the right choices?

_____
_____
_____

4) Is your inner child happy?

_____
_____
_____

5) Are you a finisher?

_____
_____
_____

6) Are you closed off from things?

7) Are you making the right decisions?

8) Are you a doer?

9) Are you making a difference?

10) Are you creating your destiny?

11) Are you determined to push through?

12) What are your desires?

_____
_____
_____

13) Are you living your dreams?

_____
_____
_____

14) Are you enthusiastic about your life?

_____
_____
_____

15) Are you energetic about your life?

_____
_____
_____

16) Are you an expert in your field?

_____
_____
_____

17) Are you excited with life?

_____
_____
_____

18) Do you know how much you want to earn this year?

19) Are you learning from the experts in your field?

20) Are you learning from your mistakes?

21) Are you continuously learning?

22) Does your life feel enriched?

23) Are you fulfilled?

24) Do you feel happy?

_____
_____
_____

25) Are you challenging yourself?

_____
_____
_____

26) Are you fit?

_____
_____
_____

27) Is your mind flexible?

_____
_____
_____

28) Is your body flexible?

_____
_____
_____

29) Are you focused about your future?

_____
_____
_____

30) Is your heart filled up?

_____
_____
_____

31) Is your mind filled with what you want?

_____
_____
_____

32) Have you faith in yourself?

_____
_____
_____

33) Are you living in gratitude?

_____
_____
_____

34) Are you growing?

_____
_____
_____

35) Are you in perfect health?

_____
_____
_____

36) Are you being really honest with yourself?

37) Are you the hero in your own life?

38) Do you know what is important right now?

39) Is your life improving?

40) Who is inspiring you?

41) Are you being your best in your job?

42) Do you love your life?

___

43) Are you leading the life you want?

___

44) Have you found your mojo?

___

45) Are you moving forward?

___

46) Have you found your niche?

___

47) Are you taking the right options?

___

48) Are you organized enough?

49) Are you getting the results you want?

50) Are you happy with the reason you are doing what you do?

51) Have you reflected on your life?

52) Are you receiving what you want from life?

53) Are you shaping your life the way you want it?

54) Do you have a big self worth?

55) Are you structured?

56) Are you taking time out?

57) Have you thought where you are in life?

58) Do you love the work you are doing?

59) Are you using your talents?

60) Do you know what you want?

_____
_____
_____

61) Do you know where you want to take your life?

_____
_____
_____

Moving forward, can you take time to answer the following questions honestly and truthfully to yourself!

1) What strategies and actions do you think you need to take?

_____
_____
_____

2) Are you aware of your emotions?

_____
_____
_____

3) Are you aware of your goals?

_____
_____
_____

4) Are you aware of your health?

_____
_____
_____

5) Are you aware of your finances?

_____
_____
_____

6) Are you aware of your faith and spirituality?

_____
_____
_____

7) Are you aware of your happiness?

_____
_____
_____

What gets written down gets brought into reality. One of the most powerful actions you can take is to write down your goals. On average, only 3% of people actually write down their goals.

Can you take the time to write down ***YOUR*** goals below?

THIS IS SO IMPORTANT!

Can you write them down in order to achieve them? When the rubber meets the road is when you write. You are present. Be specific and set a time frame.

Let go of old habits and create new ones.

Write your goals, focusing on the outcome you want to achieve. Write your goals every day.

_____
_____
_____
_____
_____
_____
_____
_____
_____
_____
_____
_____
_____
_____
_____
_____
_____
_____

Chapter 2
Action

The most important step for you to take is ACTION. The question '*What?*' has changed the life of so many people when it has been asked of them. So my '*what*' question to you is:

What will bring you from where you are now to where you want to be?

The key to this is done by using this book like a journal!

Asking yourself WHEN and WHERE brings accountability to your goals.

WHEN – The sooner you decide when you want something to change, the better. As you put pen to paper decide WHAT action you will take and WHERE your new journey begins.

I have been blessed to see thousands of people I have coached bring their lives beyond what they believed was possible. They describe their lives to me now as '*buzzing*', '*on fire*', '*phenomenal*', '*mighty*', '*brilliant*', '*in the zone*', '*fulfilled*', '*10 out of 10*', '*unreal*' and '*euphoric*'.

When will you take that first step?

Depending on your situation, this first step might be stepping up on the weighing scales, making an appointment to speak with your manager or calling that person you have been avoiding.

Each person is unique – there is only one of you. We have all been given a special unique gift.

Where you decide you really want your life to go has to start with **T I M E.**

1) What time and date will you make for this?

_____

_____

_____

2) What time will you set your alarm for?

_____

_____

_____

3) What time will you dedicate from your week to work on yourself?

_____

_____

_____

4) What time will you give yourself for what really matters?

_____

_____

_____

5) What time and date will you say 'no more' to the past?

_____

_____

_____

Now is the time to take control of your own life and decide when you will put your goals, dreams and desires into action!

Consider the following set of questions in terms of each goal, dream or desire you have. Can you sit down and answer each of the following questions honestly so that you can understand what exactly is required for you to make that dream your reality.

1) What action will you take?

_____
_____
_____

2) What new belief will you adopt?

_____
_____
_____

3) What conscious decision will you take?

_____
_____
_____

4) What energy will you bring forward?

_____
_____
_____

5) What feelings do you need to put into this?

_____
_____
_____

6) What will you focus on?

_____
_____
_____

7) What guidance will you take?

_____
_____
_____

8) What has to happen?

_____
_____
_____

9) What inspired thought will you take?

_____
_____
_____

10) What journey will you take?

_____
_____
_____

11) What knowledge do you need?

_____
_____
_____

12) What leverage will you use?

_____
_____
_____

13) What momentum will you take?

_____
_____
_____

14) How many steps will it take?

_____
_____
_____

15) What options do you have?

_____
_____
_____

16) What plans are needed?

_____
_____
_____

17) What questions need to be asked?

_____
_____
_____

18) What smart thinking needs to be done?

_____
_____
_____

19) What truth needs to be answered?

_____
_____
_____

20) What do you want the universe to provide you with?

_____
_____
_____

21) What vision do you need to see the bigger picture?

_____
_____
_____

22) Who would benefit from what you do?

_____
_____
_____

23) When will this happen?

_____
_____
_____

Chapter 3
Life Balance Wheel

To make our goals a reality, we need balance. Through my continuous coaching I have created a Life Work Balance wheel that needs to be explored in order for you to be truly fulfilled.

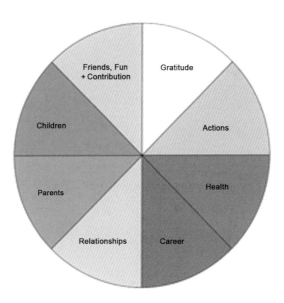

The wheel is divided into eight separate segments. The most important thing I believe from my continuous study and being a continuous student of life is that gratitude is of the highest value. When you are truly grateful for what you have, it multiplies beyond belief.

Would you agree?

For that reason, gratitude is the first segment on the wheel. Inner thoughts is the second segment on the wheel. It is my mission to help people live happier, healthier lives. Our inner thoughts of happiness and feeling good is paramount to us living our best lives.

Would you agree?

Feeling happy is something we need to be aware of. Feeling happy is something we have to work on. The quickest way to be happy is to **smile**. We can only be happy when we smile. In every different compartment of our mind, when we hold that top thought of smiling and being happy is the cornerstone to a fulfilled life.

My clients and friends have told me that the continuous awareness through reading their wheels daily, reminds them to keep focus on smiling and being grateful.

Would you agree?

Feeling good, great, amazing, brilliant, excited, happy and inspired are all ways we can feel fulfilled. If you get a thought that doesn't make you feel good, can I ask you to be aware that this is a reminder for you to change this to a good / happy wish?

I am now going to empower you to make a change by asking a series of '*Can you*' questions. Now is the time to put your pen to paper and commit yourself to making changes.

Please either *tick* or write *yes* after the questions below if you agree.

1) Can I continue improving being grateful for my health?

2) Can I continue improving being grateful for my intelligence?

3) Can I continue improving being grateful for my manners?

4) Can I continue improving being grateful for my self-esteem?

5) Can I continue improving being grateful for my trust?

6) Can I continue improving being grateful for my positive thoughts?

7) Can I continue improving being grateful for beliefs?

8) Can I continue improving being aware of each moment?

9) Can I continue improving appreciation for all that is good in my life?

10) Can I continue improving being my best?

11) Can I continue improving being confident?

12) Can I continue improving being in control of my life?

13) Can I continue improving following my dreams?

14) Can I continue improving being fun?

15) Can I continue improving being happy?

16) Can I continue improving being kind?

17) Can I continue improving loving myself?

18) Can I continue improving listening to my thoughts?

19) Can I continue improving serving my needs?

20) Can I continue improving my intelligence?

21) Can I continue improving my independence?

22) Can I continue improving my learning?

23) Can I continue improving my life?

24) Can I continue improving my openness?

25) Can I continue improving my being strong?

26) Can I continue improving my smiling?

27) Can I continue improving my being truthful?

28) Can I continue improving my uniqueness?

29) Can I continue improving valuing myself?

Chapter 4
Perfect Health

The two top most important things people rate is their happiness and their health. For this reason, perfect health is the third segment on the wheel. It is third to place emphasis on the fact that without good health we cannot truly achieve any goal.

This segment was originally called good health but it was renamed to perfect health because you become what you tell yourself most of the time.

When you have a powerful thought process about perfect health and then if you front-load it with 'I am happy and grateful for my perfect health', there is a powerful alignment between your mind and body.

I have been lucky to see with my own two eyes that this incantation done consistently transforms people's health to perfect health.

1) Can I continue improving my breath?

2) Can I continue improving on being an athlete?

3) Can I continue improving my balanced diet?

4) Can I continue improving making the right choices?

5) Can I continue improving cleansing my body?

6) Can I continue improving drinking 2 to 3 litres of water or more per day?

7) Can I continue improving exercising for 20 to 30 minutes or more a day, 5 days a week or more?

8) Can I continue improving being fit?

9) Can I continue improving feeling good about my body?

10) Can I continue improving eating healthy?

11) Can I continue improving having good healthy habits?

12) Can I continue improving listening to my body?

13) Can I continue improving loving my body?

14) Can I continue improving being disciplined about what I put into my body?

15) Can I continue improving relaxing my body?

16) Can I continue improving smiling through my body?

17) Can I continue improving being strong?

18) Can I continue improving being centered?

19) Can I continue improving allowing my body to shine?

20) Can I continue improving toning my body?

21) Can I continue improving being vibrant?

22) Can I continue improving being vitalized?

Chapter 5
Career

This is so important! I have a deep belief that when we find our gift in the career path we choose, we don't work anymore, we play.

The most successful people in business spend 80% of their time playing on their top strengths and the remaining 20% on areas that aren't their strengths, which in itself is a strength.

My challenge to you is to think deep and ask yourself:

1) What are your strengths?

_____
_____
_____

2) How can you use these to your best ability?

_____
_____
_____

When people I have worked with have zoned in on this area and realized where their true strength lies, instead of trying to do everything in their career / business, they have delegated the areas that aren't their top strengths. This has completely transformed their businesses and their careers. Can you take a few moments to ask yourself the following questions and see what resonates with you.

1) Can I continue improving my attitude towards my work?

2) Can I continue improving doing my best at my work?

3) Can I continue improving being creative at my work?

4) Can I continue improving enjoying my work?

5) Can I continue improving being a finisher at my work?

6) Can I continue improving reaching my goals at my work?

7) Can I continue improving being innovative at my work?

8) Can I continue improving being giving during my work time?

9) Can I continue improving being a master at my work?

10) Can I continue improving taking correct options at my work?

11) Can I continue improving availing of the best opportunities at my work?

12) Can I continue improving taking pleasure from my work?

13) Can I continue improving being professional about my work?

14) Can I continue improving knowing and seeing my potential at my work?

Chapter 6
Best Partner / Best Self / Relationship

If you currently do not have a partner, can you use this segment to focus on being your best self.

The key to this segment is to understand your partner's world. Create time to share with them (or yourself). Many people have let go or forgotten about the romance part of their relationship as years go by, however it is extremely important to keep the flames alive.

My question to you is:

When did you have your last date?

Allowing your partner to grow and express him or herself is extremely important. It is important to appreciate your partner's greatness.

Can you write down 10 great things about your partner?

_____
_____
_____
_____
_____
_____
_____
_____
_____
_____
_____

Can you write down 10 things your partner has done for you that you are grateful for:

_____
_____
_____
_____
_____
_____
_____
_____
_____
_____

Can you now write 10 things you might not have thanked your partner for?

_____
_____
_____
_____
_____
_____
_____
_____
_____
_____

1) Can I continue improving being accepting of my partner?

2) Can I continue improving being acknowledging of my partner?

3) Can I continue improving being affectionate with my partner?

4) Can I continue improving being communicative with my partner?

5) Can I continue improving being caring of my partner?

6) Can I continue improving being expressive towards my partner?

7) Can I continue improving empowering my partner?

8) Can I continue improving being grateful for my partner?

9) Can I continue improving being forgiving of my partner?

10) Can I continue improving being fulfilled with my partner?

11) Can I continue improving having fun with my partner?

12) Can I continue improving being generous with my partner?

13) Can I continue improving being honest with my partner?

14) Can I continue improving being intimate with my partner?

15) Can I continue improving being interested in my partner?

16) Can I continue improving being loving towards my partner?

17) Can I continue improving listening to my partner?

18) Can I continue improving being open with my partner?

19) Can I continue improving being patient with my partner?

20) Can I continue improving being romantic with my partner?

21) Can I continue improving relating to my partner?

22) Can I continue improving being tuned in to my partner?

23) Can I continue improving being understanding of my partner?

24) Can I continue improving being reflective with my partner?

Chapter 7

Best Parent

Our responsibility being a parent is to bring our children up in the happiest and most confident way possible. Be your best by supporting, encouraging, guiding and listening to them.

Make sure you understand them and their world. Show them empathy and compassion.

1) Can you rate yourself out of 10 at being a parent?

_____

2) If it is not a 10, what do you think has to happen to get it to a 10?

_____
_____
_____

Do you need to listen more?

Do you need to guide more?

Do you need to show more love?

Do you need to talk more?

Do you need to educate more?

Do you need to have more empathy?

Do you need to have more compassion?

Do you need to praise more?

Do you need to thank more?

Do you need to encourage more?

3) Are you spending enough time with them?

___

4) When is this time?

___

5) How long do you spend with them?

___

6) Create your own family time by defining:

How long you will spend together?

Where!
When!
What you all will do!

Move away from technology (televisions, telephones, etcetera) to spend quality time.

Now is your time to make these important decisions.

7) Can I continue improving loving my children?

8) Can I continue improving connecting with my children?

9) Can I continue improving encouraging my children?

10) Can I continue improving playing with my children?

11) Can I continue improving laughing with my children?

12) Can I continue improving teaching my children through encouragement?

13) Can I continue improving connecting with my children's passions?

14) Can I continue improving helping my children improve their good daily habits?

15) Can I continue improving planning and having adventures with my children?

16) Can I continue improving creating magic moments with my children?

17) Can I continue improving believing in my children?

18) Can I continue improving challenging my children?

19) Can I continue improving exercising with my children?

20) Can I continue improving empowering my children with my positive language?

21) Can I continue improving enlightening my children?

22) Can I continue improving having faith in my children?

23) Can I continue improving knowing my children's friends?

24) Can I continue improving being interested in my children's hobbies?

25) Can I continue improving helping my children heal from their hurts?

26) Can I continue improving helping my children use their intelligence?

27) Can I continue improving encouraging my children to use their imagination?

28) Can I continue improving being disciplined as a parent?

29) Can I continue improving being compassionate as a parent?

30) Can I continue improving being forgiving as a parent?

31) Can I continue improving being honest as a parent?

32) Can I continue improving being influential as a parent?

33) Can I continue improving being inspirational as a parent?

34) Can I continue improving creating happy memories as a parent?

35) Can I continue improving being open as a parent?

36) Can I continue improving having time as a parent?

37) Can I continue improving my friendship as a parent?

Chapter 8

Best Son / Daughter / Brother / Sister

We have to be appreciative of the time that others spent on us. Our parents have done the best they could with the tools and resources they had.

Many relationships are not perfect. Perhaps there may be hurt that goes back many years, much of this was unintentional. The key here is to let those hurts go. Heal and forgive if it needs to be forgiven. So many people transform their lives when they unblock this area.

This is what I have found from working with people when they have done this.

The same applies to our brothers and sisters. The two **magic words** here are: *Forgive* and *Heal*. If you forgive and heal yourself, you can move forward.

1) Out of 10, how is your relationship with your parents?

    _____

2) If your parents have passed, you can still continue to love them or forgive them if you feel you need to.

    The same applies to any siblings. How is your relationship with them now? More importantly!

3) How good a brother / sister are **YOU** to them?

    _____

The number one thing parents love the most is when their children stay in touch. Have you been in touch with your parents recently?

4) Can I continue improving my appreciation for all my parents have done for me?

5) Can I continue improving acknowledging my parents and brothers / sisters?

6) Can I continue improving giving acceptance to my parents and brothers / sisters?

7) Can I continue improving caring for my parents and brothers / sisters?

8) Can I continue improving my cheerfulness around my parents and brothers / sisters?

9) Can I continue improving communication with my parents and brothers / sisters?

10) Can I continue improving my levels of compassion for my parents and brothers / sisters?

11) Can I continue improving complimenting my parents and brothers / sisters?

12) Can I continue improving encouraging my parents and brothers / sisters?

13) Can I continue improving the fun I have with my parents and brothers / sisters?

14) Can I continue improving forgiving my parents and brothers / sisters?

15) Can I continue improving being generous with my parents and brothers / sisters?

16) Can I continue improving giving to my parents and brothers / sisters?

17) Can I continue improving being grateful for my parents and brothers / sisters?

18) Can I continue improving being honest with my parents and brothers / sisters?

19) Can I continue improving being interested in my parents and brothers / sisters?

20) Can I continue improving inspiring my parents and brothers / sisters?

21) Can I continue improving being kind to my parents and brothers / sisters?

22) Can I continue improving the love I have for my parents and brothers / sisters?

23) Can I continue improving laughing with my parents and brothers / sisters?

24) Can I continue improving learning from my parents and brothers / sisters?

25) Can I continue improving being open with my parents and brothers / sisters?

26) Can I continue improving being patient with my parents and brothers / sisters?

27) Can I continue improving being respectful to my parents and brothers / sisters?

28) Can I continue improving being sincere with my parents and brothers / sisters?

29) Can I continue improving being thankful around my parents and brothers / sisters?

30) Can I continue improving being truthful when with my parents and brothers / sisters?

31) Can I continue improving staying in touch with my parents and brothers / sisters?

32) Can I continue improving the time I spend with my parents and brothers / sisters?

33) Can I continue improving understanding their era?

34) Can I continue improving valuing my parents and brothers / sisters?

35) Can I continue improving giving a warm welcome to my parents and brothers / sisters?

Chapter 9
Friends, Fun and Contribution

My sincere belief is that we are here two times, one time and a good time. So many successful people have come to me that are a 10 on their career segment of the wheel but do not feel fulfilled.

Fulfillment is an art – that art can be achieved if you truly allow yourself to enjoy your life. Truly enjoy everyday, including today. **ENJOY THIS DAY, THIS MOMENT.** Can I ask you right now to enjoy this moment as you let these words sink in?

Can you take a few moments to reflect on the following! Can you make a commitment to allow even more joy into each moment?

    In terms of contribution:

    Are you involved in your community?
    Are you involved in a sport?
    Do you volunteer?

As the secret to living is giving, how can you give even more?

1)   Can I continue to appreciate my friends?

2)   Can I continue improving my awareness around my friends?

3)   Can I continue improving staying in touch with friends?

4)   Can I continue having adventure with my friends?

5) Can I continue improving my level of connectedness with my friends?

6) Can I continue improving my courageness?

7) Can I continue improving my contribution to society?

8) Can I continue improving my contribution to my friends?

9) Can I continue improving my contribution to fun activities?

10) Can I continue improving my levels of fun?

11) Can I continue improving at my hobbies?

12) Can I continue improving my level of interest in my friends?

13) Can I continue improving laughing with my friends?

14) Can I continue making long lasting happy memories with my friends?

15) Can I continue making long lasting contributions to society?

Chapter 10
Putting it all together

You have all this knowledge now that you have searched deep within yourself throughout this book. I want to take this time to congratulate you and honour your commitment to follow through.

I know at this stage you will have massive clarity and you will have discovered where you are and what you really want through this journey of self-discovery.

Now is the time for even more action – to create your own personal life balance wheel. Can I take this opportunity to remind you that you are a beautiful shining diamond both inside and out? You are totally unique, born with your talents and gifts. Can you now use this time to fill in your own life balance wheel?

The life balance wheel is on the next page, so starting with segment one, Gratitude – I want you to write in the Top 5 things you are grateful for. Some suggestions could include:

* Being Alive
* Your Happiness
* Your Health
* Your Family
* Your Attitude
* Your Gratefulness

My Balance Wheel

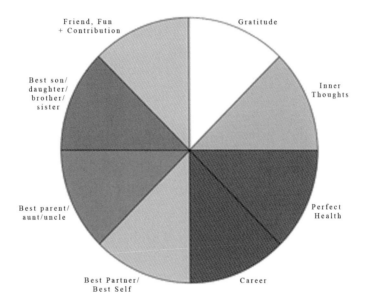

Next fill in your Top 5 Inner Thoughts. People's big search in their lives is for more happiness. I have been asked over and over how do we achieve this? I am now going to tell you the three quickest ways to be happier in your life:

1) Smile
2) Be Grateful
3) Have Good Thoughts

For this section write in the inner thoughts you have that make you smile and happy. Some suggestions for this segment include:

- Hold onto a thought that makes you continuously smile
- Be continuously grateful
- Continuously focus on only the good things in our lives
- Focus on the good that you are going to create in your own life
- Focus on how you can bring happiness to others

Next fill in your Top 5 in terms of your Perfect Health. These are things you can do to bring your health to the next level.

Suggestions here include:

- Hydration (Drink 3 to 4 litres of water per day)
- Make healthy food choices
- Try for 20+ minutes exercise 5 days a week
- Give yourself some Me-Time for mediation and relaxation
- Flexibility Work – yoga, stretches, etcetera

When filling in your Top 5 for the Career segment, make sure you really align these to your strengths. Suggestions here include:

- Be prepared everyday before turning up to work
- Be fully committed
- Continuously master your craft
- Look at your role as benefiting someone else's life

The next segment, Best Partner – can be filled in as Best Self if you are single. Some suggestions for segment 5 include:

- List 5 great things about your Partner
- Focus on the their greatness
- Listen and understand their world
- Spend / create quality time with them
- Have fun and enjoy the time you spend with them

Segment 6, Best Parent – can be filled out next. If you are not a parent, use this segment as Best Uncle / Aunt to cover any time you spend with children in your life. Suggestions for this segment include:

- Appreciate them
- Show empathy and compassion
- Understand their world – meet them at their level
- Continuously educate them
- Enjoy and cherish these magic moments with them

The second last segment, Best Son / Daughter – allows you to discover your role in the family you were born into. Use this segment to write your Top 5 in terms of your parents, your brother, sisters and grandparents. Suggestions here include:

- Focus on their good qualities
- Appreciate them
- Stay in touch
- Connect with their passions
- Enjoy them

The last segment, Friends, Fun and Contribution – allows you to write the ways in which you can have fun and contribute to your community. Suggestions for this segment include:

- The Secret to Living is Giving
- Give to charity
- Volunteer
- Stay in touch with friends
- Give back to the local community

Now that you have filled out your life balance wheel, can I tell you about learning? The reason I asked you to write out your life balance wheel is so you can learn at 100% capacity. When we are told something, we learn 10%. When a third party demonstrates something, we learn at 50% capacity. When we are involved ourselves, we learn at 90%.

You have been involved 90% because every time you have written and questioned yourself throughout this book you have been involved and immersed in your own life. Every time you put pen to paper on this book, every time you looked deep into your world and your life, you were involved and engaged.

The golden key to the last 10% is obtained through continuous commitment to follow through in reading the specific pages that you have written in on a daily basis. Can you do this at least 5 times a week?

As we are made up of mind, body and soul, the majority of people focus solely on the middle part, the body. We can keep our body fit and muscular by going to the gym. This is all great but if we look back to what comes first it is our **mind**.

The **mind** controls everything that we do! What we tell our minds we become! I have been very lucky to have coached many people from all walks of life through this specific process which I am going to share with you now – Mind Gym Time.

Some people have called it " *Their Mind JIM Time*" It is really up to you as to how you see it. Your Mind Gym Time, when used correctly is the golden key to open and operate your life to its full potential. So how does this work?

MY MIND GYM TIME

> When?
> Where?
> How Long?

All studies show our mind is most receptive to our creative thoughts last at night and first thing in the morning. Can you take the time now to flick back over your own handwritten notes in this book / journal and earmark each page you have written on.

Create a place or space for you to do this in your life daily. Allow yourself 10, 15 or 20 minutes, whichever feels right for you. My big promise that I make to you is that the more time and energy you put into these magic creative moments, the more fulfillment, happiness, joy and success you will bring to yourself.

The commitment you make to your Mind Gym Time will equal the phenomenal quality of your life.

Further Support

If you would like to contact me, I would be grateful to help in any way that I can.

    email: **jimhickeyglobal@gmail.com**
    website: **www.jimhickeyglobal.com**

I would love for you to email me when you have completed your journaling as I know it's the follow through that makes a massive difference. This is what brings me the most joy.

Log on to **www.jimhickeyglobal.com/** For links to:

* Confident Happy Children, The Books of A B C Steps
* Blank Balance Wheel Download
* Meditation Music
* Video link to clips from Mind Gym Seminar
* Subscribe to monthly newsletter of advice, tips and hints

Thank you. Thank you. Thank you.

Warmest,

Jim